Never on Wednesday
the first decade of the Rio Grande Zephyr

Richard Loveman
Mel Patrick

contents

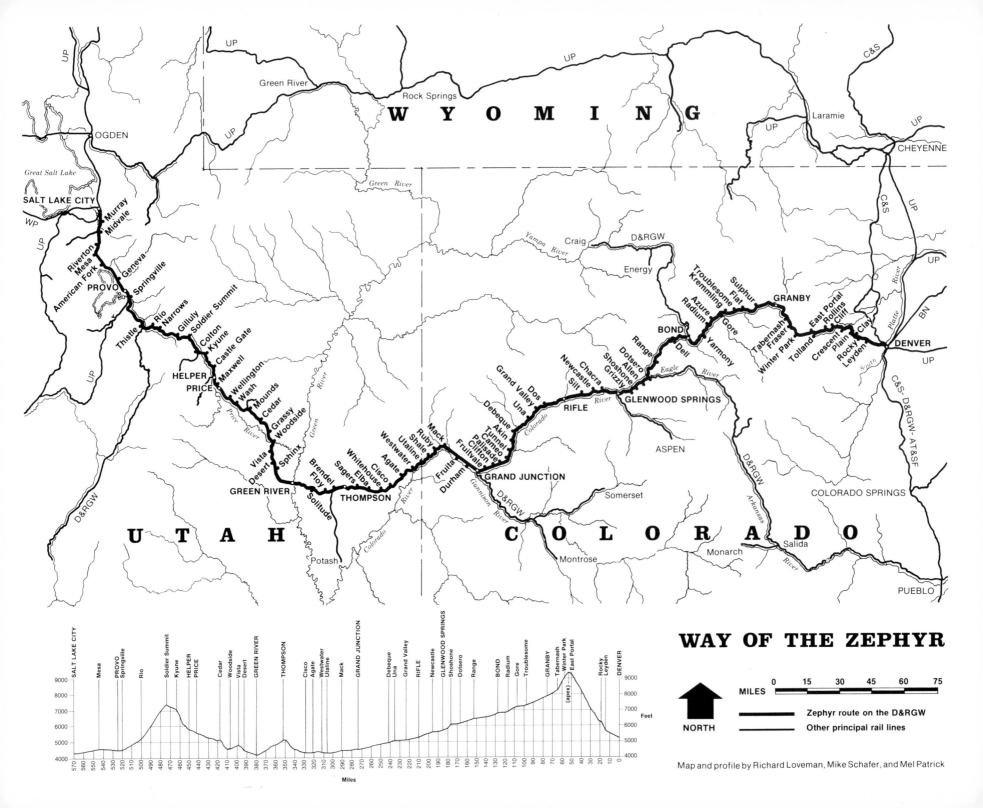

WAY OF THE ZEPHYR

MILES
0   15   30   45   60   75

━━━━━ Zephyr route on the D&RGW

───── Other principal rail lines

NORTH

Map and profile by Richard Loveman, Mike Schafer, and Mel Patrick

ISSUED AUGUST 2, 1979

TIMETABLES

DENVER • GLENWOOD SPRINGS • GRAND JUNCTION
SALT LAKE CITY • OGDEN

READ DOWN			READ UP
No. 17			**No. 18**
Monday Thursday Saturday	Miles	RIO GRANDE ZEPHYR TRI-WEEKLY (Mountain Time)	Tuesday Friday Sunday
7:30 AM	0	Lv. Denver, Colo. . . . . . . Ar.	9:30 PM
9:55 AM	75	Lv. Granby . . . . ♦Lv.	6:50 PM
11:30 AM	129	Lv. Bond . . . . ♦Lv.	5:20 PM
1:10 PM	185	Lv. Glenwood Springs . . Lv.	3:40 PM
1:40 PM	212	Lv. Rifle . . . . ♦Lv.	3:05 PM
2:55 PM	275	Ar. Grand Junction . . . . Lv.	1:55 PM
3:10 PM	275	Lv. Grand Junction . . . . Ar.	1:40 PM
x 4:30 PM	353	Lv. Thompson, Utah . . . ♦Lv.	x12:10 AM
f 4:55 PM	380	Lv. Green River . . . . . . ♦Lv.	f11:45 AM
6:20 PM	451	Lv. Helper . . . . ♦Lv.	10:30 AM
8:25 PM	526	Lv. Provo . . . . ♦Lv.	8:20 AM
9:30 PM	570	Ar. Salt Lake City . . . . . Lv.	7:30 AM
9:40 PM	570	Lv. Salt Lake City (Note A)Ar.	7:20 AM
10:30 PM	607	Ar. Ogden, Utah (Note A) ♦Lv.	6:30 AM

NOTE A: Limousine between Salt Lake City and Ogden for revenue passengers from or to points east of Salt Lake City, and revenue passengers arriving or departing Ogden on Amtrak train to or from Salt Lake City or east. No local passengers handled between Salt Lake City and Ogden.

♦ No checked baggage handled at this station.

x Stops on flag to discharge revenue passengers, also to receive revenue passengers holding advance reservations.

f Stops on flag to discharge revenue passengers, also to receive revenue passengers holding advance reservations on notification to Agent, Thompson, or Helper, Utah.

EQUIPMENT
Vista Dome Chair Car, Chair Car, Vista Dome Lounge, Dining Car, between Denver and Salt Lake City.
Coach Seat Reservations Required

For Additional Information See Other Side

D&RGW public timetable dated August 2, 1979, courtesy D&RGW. Schedules subject to change.

introduction

THE PASSENGER train industry in the years following World War II was like a supernova: It exploded brightly and with great promise, then quickly succumbed. Nearly as soon as troop sleepers had been tucked into storage, American railroads began knocking at the doors of Budd, Pullman-Standard, and other builders with the good news that it was time to revamp the nation's passenger trains for the optimistic years ahead. Soon the likes of Chicago, New York, San Francisco, Dallas, Cincinnati, and St. Louis were linked by a marvelous array of new or reborn stars: from *Pere Marquette* to *Panama Limited*, from *City of Portland* to *South Wind*.

The decline of all this happiness was an accelerating function, and it was only a matter of time before what remained of the American rail passenger network by the end of the 1960s was thrown into the lap of the government. The result was the National Railroad Passenger Corporation, better known as Amtrak. Although Amtrak eventually reversed the trend of declining passenger train patronage against seemingly overwhelming odds, it was accomplished with bitter medicine for the many diehard proponents of passenger train travel: passenger trains became individual in name only as new look-alike, utilitarian Amfleet and Superliner cars rolled off assembly lines to become the mainstay of all American intercity passenger trains.

Ah, but while Amtrak took to task rejuvenating America's passenger trains as economics, funding, and politics dictated, there remained a silver-lined reminder of those colorful passenger trains of the Forties, Fifties, and Sixties: Denver & Rio Grande Western's *Rio Grande Zephyr*. The irony is that the RGZ was born in the 1970's, although it featured equipment that was, in fact, constructed immediately after World War II.

As a Vista-Dome stainless steel streamliner with a schedule tailored for daytime service to a specific region, the RGZ was unique to the 1970s, but it did not exist in a vacuum of tradition. Specifically there were two classic prototypes for this type of daylight domeliner service: Chicago, Burlington & Quincy's seven-car *Twin Cities Zephyrs* of 1947 between Chicago and Minneapolis, and Wabash Railroad's six-car domeliner *Blue Bird* which premiered on the Chicago-St. Louis run in 1950.

Generally, the domed versions of these trains, built by the Budd Company of Philadelphia, included a combine, three or four Vista-Dome coaches, a dining car, and a dome parlor-observation-lounge. As you peruse the scenes of this book and note the dome-studded consist of the *Rio Grande Zephyr*, its link with those long-vanished classics becomes quite graphic.

The operation of the *Rio Grande Zephyr* was very different from that of its *California Zephyr* ancestor, inaugurated in 1949 and discontinued in 1970. The RGZ should not be viewed as a sleeperless mutant of that famous train. True, there were a myriad of holdovers from the days of the CZ, not the least of which were the cars and locomotives, but there was a major difference: cross-country traffic was virtually non-existent aboard the RGZ; indeed, there were few through passengers between its terminal cities, Denver and Salt Lake.

The *California Zephyr* was a joint service among three railroads. In contrast, the *Rio Grande Zephyr* was a homeroad-bound train, and so in some ways could be considered as much a descendant of D&RGW's famous *Prospector* on the overnight Denver-Salt Lake City run as it was a descendant of the CZ. The RGZ's operation, personnel, and service standards were in the Rio Grande heritage of that well-liked train of the 1950s and 1960s, which in some respects made the *Rio Grande Zephyr* a living ghost of the *Prospector*.

When Amtrak was created in 1971, the *Rio Grande*

Zephyr became notable as being one of the few remaining privately operated traditional passenger trains in the continental U.S., a distinction it shared with Rock Island's two remaining *Rockets* and Southern's *Piedmont, Asheville Special,* and *Southern Crescent.* However, by the close of the 1970s the *Rockets* had wandered into oblivion (very nearly, along with their railroad) as had the *Asheville Special* and *Piedmont,* and the *Southern Crescent* wore Amtrak's red, white, and blue. Now the RGZ was more than just a notable. It had become the last of the last.

It was notable for other "lasts" too. The equipment assigned to the RGZ included the last of the EMD F-unit-type locomotives used in intercity passenger service, the last of the Alco passenger locomotives (though converted solely for steam-generator utility), and the last matched set of post World War II passenger cars.

There is another tradition that was part of the *Rio Grande Zephyr* experience—that of the D&RGW and its long history of tourist-oriented passenger services. Rio Grande is synonymous with narrow gauge, and certainly the road's 3-foot gauge, steam-powered Durango-Silverton operation was foremost in the tourist railroad industry. But scenery and tourists have long played a significant part of Rio Grande's standard-gauge passenger service too. Recall, if you will, Rio Grande's enduring custom of pausing its Pueblo route daylight passenger trains for 10 minutes at the middle of the Royal Gorge of the Arkansas River solely for the tourists to absorb the grandeur of the scenery. The practice revealed Rio Grande's reverence for the awesome handiwork of an ultimate Creator.

Tourists are not necessarily sightseers either. Rocky Mountain snows annually provide reason for D&RGW to run ski trains, a tradition that has been all but lost in other parts of the country. Denver-Winter Park Ski Specials tromped out of Denver Union Terminal on the trail of the *Rio Grande Zephyr* into the 1980s.

If tourism was one of the RGZ's links to the past, then it was also the train's main link to survival. Business travelers had all but abandoned rail travel in favor of the skies above, but the RGZ successfully continued its designed function as a tourist carrier catering to that segment of Denver's population in search of a scenic, leisurely way to get from A to B (in this case, A being Denver, and B, Glenwood Springs). The surprising twist to the tourist nature of the train was that all such traffic was generated out of the 1970s; little of it was inherited from the CZ, which hosted primarily cross-country travelers in search of a scenic way to roll from Chicago to the West Coast. The proof is in RGZ's growth: In the early 1970s it was but a four-car train, but by the time train-riders rang in the 1980s, eight- and nine-car trains were the norm.

The worldwide energy problem was perhaps the single most important ticket to the continued success of the *Rio Grande Zephyr,* and with this in mind, the train schedule theoretically could exist indefinitely. However, the 25-year-old locomotives and 30-year-old rolling stock have gently aged through the years, and even D&RGW's diligent maintenance program can only prolong the life of the equipment for a few more years. Further, rail passenger operations are seldom economically successful, no matter how many seats are filled with satisfied customers, so at the time of this writing no one could know how long the *Rio Grand Zephyr* would physically exist.

But then the contents of this volume are neither about the mechanics nor the future—nor for that matter the history—of the *Rio Grande Zephyr.* The scope of the work herein includes those items, people, and places that formed the *Rio Grande Zephyr* experience, and the purpose of the work is to record the comings and goings of this last of the once ubiquitous *Zephyrs.*

In general the photos are organized into geographic sequence, from east to west, along the route of the RGZ. Environment and habitat tell much about a train's character traits, and in that sense this book is also a study of the lands, the towns, and the D&RGW right of way between Denver and Salt Lake City.

For the book's photographers there are many memories and sensations to be remembered in the years of tracking the *Zephyr.* Most don't show within the black and white prints: waiting in the sizzling sun atop a barren cliff overlooking Ruby Canyon, bracing against the frigid winter winds of Fraser while waiting at trackside for the *Zephyr,* chasing the eastbound RGZ up Soldier Summit on a clear Sunday morning when the road was yours, the predictable and quite audible approach of 5771 and friends wending their way between narrow canyon walls, and watching the train's passage through the camera viewfinder forgetting for a moment (again) that the rest of the U.S. passenger train world was Amtrak.

For those of you who never had the opportunity to watch the canyon walls of Gore, Ruby, and others slip past the dome windows of Silver Sky or to dine on Rocky Mountain Trout in *Silver Banquet* as the waters of the Colorado River glimmered outside your window, we trust that this book will bring you into the world of the *Rio Grande Zephyr.* For those of you fortunate enough to have ridden this unique little train, we hope that this book will help you to recall those pleasant moments with vivid clarity. And for all of you who are interested, who want to remember, the following pages are presented.

Richard Loveman
Mel Patrick
Denver, Colorado

March 1980

1

climb to Moffat

PLEASE answer this question, dear reader, even if you've never laid eyes on D&RGW trains 17 and 18: What comes to mind when you think, *Rio Grande Zephyr*? To many the name means relaxed travel, comradery, good cuisine. But chances are you're in the majority if you equate the train with the superb scenery that is its habitat, especially from Denver westward through the Front Range to the Moffat Tunnel.

Not that the landscapes are better in those first 50 miles than at any other portion of the *Zephyr's* 570-mile Denver-Salt Lake City trip. No, not on a ride whose prelude is Denver's endless suburbia. Rather, it's the *transition* from metropolis to wilderness, from flatlands to uplands that makes this segment so memorable. And what makes it downright spectacular is that the transition is not gradual—the Front Range of the Colorado Rockies juts up from the plains like great walls guarding a palace, and the D&RGW main line must rise more than 100 feet every mile to surmount those walls. To witness the *Zephyr's* grinding climb along track that loops through foothills and then grapples mountain faces was to witness railroading drama at its best.

The *Rio Grande Zephyr's* mostly daylight, tailored-for-tourists schedule was in essence inherited from its predecessor, *California Zephyr*, along with other legacies including domes, dining and lounge service, and dedicated crews. Missing, though, were the through passengers that boarded CZ cars at the likes of Chicago Union Station, Oakland, and Omaha. Denver-Glenwood Springs was the stonghold of Rio Grande's passenger market of the 1970s.

Happily, some things never change. During the 1970s, as in the CZ years, passengers still clambered for dome seats upon departure from Denver—front row seats for scenery that was "among the best in the West", as Zephyrettes once touted over CZ P.A. systems when their train rolled out of the Mile High City on D&RGW track. Few could argue the claim considering the magnificent vistas that have entranced travelers since June 23, 1904, when the first scheduled passenger train of David Moffat's erstwhile Denver, Northwestern & Pacific steamed out of Denver for what today is known as Tolland, near the east end of Moffat Tunnel. So, the thrill of the climb to the Divide was a tradition that long predates the CZ and Moffat Tunnel; it was an experience that awakened the pioneer spirit in all who travel for the sake of travel.

R.L.

still a gateway

Denver Union Station looms at the foot of Seventeenth Street on the northwest side of downtown Denver. The career for this once-bustling gateway between the Rockies and the Great Plains reached a low point on May 1, 1971, when, with the advent of Amtrak, well-remembered flagships such as the *City of Denver* arrived for the final time. For the duration of the 1970s, Union Station's rail traffic remained somewhat constant: one daily Amtrak *Zephyr* in each direction, the tri-weekly *Rio Grande Zephyr,* and an occasional special train.

Nearly vacant platforms on the other side of Union Station's ornate facade indicate that most passengers are aboard Rio Grande's goodwill conveyance as 7:30 a.m. departure time nears. Vista-Dome observation-lounge *Silver Sky,* sans its neon *California Zephyr* drumhead, brings up the markers of this regulatory remnant they call the *Rio Grande Zephyr.*

M.P.

R.L.

R.L.

R.L.

In spite of the moderate number of trains using the facility, there was always a certain amount of quickened station activity at dawn on the days that the *Zephyr* went west, as the four scenes on this page show.

13

Denver departures

In at least one rare instance during the 1970s, the *Rio Grande Zephyr* departed Denver in the company of a blizzard-delayed Amtrak train 6, the *San Francisco Zephyr*. On track 2, sandwiched between the two *Zephyrs*, is a Winter Park ski train that will follow D&RGW 17 out of the depot by five minutes. The more typical lineup during the predawn hours of a short January day (facing page) has the *Rio Grande Zephyr* waiting to depart for Salt Lake City on track 1 while the Winter Park Ski Special stretches out on track 2.

prospects are good

Before No. 17 could literally head west toward the mountains, it had to clear terminal yard trackage and pick up train orders at Prospect Junction. Here in July 1979, continuing a 30-year-old ritual for west-of-Denver *Zephyrs*, No. 17, with business car *Wilson McCarthy* on the rear, eases over Colorado & Southern trackage past Prospect's train-order station while conductor and brakeman snag orders "on the fly."

R.L.

westward ho!

Once clear of the junction trackage, the *Zephyr* accelerated out of the Platte River valley on home trackage. In the February 1977 scene at left, Pueblo-bound Rio Grande freight No. 65 holds for the *Zephyr* just south of Rio Grande's North Yard. In the January scene below, recorded during the last year of the 1970s, the *Zephyr* makes a rolling pass with the Winter Park Ski Special at Leyden, the first siding west of Denver. Typically, the ski train departed Union Station after the *Zephyr*.

R.L.

R.L.

Front Range formalities

On the facing page, eastbound No. 36, a hot overnight freight from Salt Lake City, impatiently waits for the *Zephyr* to clear the east turnout of Rocky siding in January 1976. Rocky is located at the east (or bottom) end of the well-known series of 10-degree curves known as the Big Ten. At right the westbound *Zephyr* climbs between the two 10-degree turnback curves that lift the D&RGW main line through the foothills and onto the Front Range. Eastbound trains drifting down from the Front Range receive an advance indication from the unusual dual-target CTC signal at the west end of Rocky siding.

R.L.

R.L.

R.L.

round 'n round at Rocky

Now join us at other vantage points to witness westbound varnish ascending Big Ten. On the facing page No. 17 negotiates the lower swoop of Big Ten, and at left the train grinds out of the tangent of track connecting the lower loop with the upper; moments later it would pass along the highest level of track in the background at Clay siding. Above, F units on the Sunday version of the popular ski train wheel the ex-*Prospector* combine and eight ancient ex-Northern Pacific coaches through the lower loop. Now and then the ski train rated the F-unit/steam-generator power normally assigned to the *Zephyr*. On this occasion the 11-car Moffat Tunnel 50th Anniversary run of the *Rio Grande Zephyr* required the muscle of three freight units, which bumped the F's to the ski train.

M.P.

M.P.

your tickets, please

The Zephyr's veteran conductors always took their charge seriously, but they were always ready to answer the seemingly endless stream of questions, trade a smile, or exchange rail stories. Here conductor Jim Wood and another crewman tend to their bookkeeping in the dome as the westbound Zephyr climbs out of the flatlands. Down in the diner it's "Second call to breakfast!" as waiters serve famous Rio Grande French Toast and Bloody Marys to morning dining car guests.

R.L.

M.P.

Above Big Ten loops the D&RGW main line twists and bends through numerous reverse curves to strengthen its foothold on the Front Range. Below, No. 17 climbs the north slope of Coal Creek Canyon before curling into Tunnel 1.

following pages

In this sequence photographed in June 1980, the westbound *Zephyr* has just cleared the west turnout of Clay siding (first photo) and is about to swing into the mouth of Coal Creek Canyon to gain more elevation. Moments later (second photo) the train briefly heads eastward after exiting the canyon and Tunnel 1. R.L.

R.L.

M.P.

M.P.

M.P.

To reach a canyon whose contours permit easy penetration all the way to the Continental Divide, the D&RGW main line must climb northward along the face of the Front Range to the mouth of South Boulder Canyon. During this 2 per cent ascent, *Rio Grande Zephyr* passengers are treated to breathtaking vistas interspersed by short cliffhanging tunnels. Above, No. 17 noses through Rainbow Cut on the main track at Plainview siding. The facing page presents a graphic illustration of the tunnel stitching as Rio Grande's glamour girl threads in and out of the morning sunshine.

M.P.

During the 1970s there were few items of civilization that maintained an absolute continuity with the past. The *Rio Grande Zephyr* was an exception. Perennially satisfying the railroad's public relations requirements, if not their fiscal ones, the *Zephyr* provided uncountable goodwill memories for those who booked passage aboard the dome train. Below, two kids discover the exhilaration of a vestibule ride. At left, domefuls of riders absorb the views as No. 17 cuts along and sometimes through the escarpments of the Front Range.

her majesty in majesty

High above the private community of Eldorado Springs the D&RGW main line leaves the face of the Front Range and dives west into the Rockies, seeking the path of least resistance—the canyon of South Boulder Creek—toward Moffat Tunnel. At right, in the canyon, No. 17 approaches the mouth of Tunnel 10 while passengers catch a last look at the city of Boulder and the Great Plains stretching off to the horizon. Below, domes, diner, and obs gracefully slip away from the mouth of Tunnel 3.

M.P.

M.P.

R.L.

The twisting, tunnel-laden climb of the *Zephyr* is interrupted by the passing track at milepost 31.2, known as Crescent. An 8-car *Rio Grande Zephyr* led by the usual assortment of winter power, above right, glides along the main track at Crescent and, below right, disappears around the curve at the west switch of the siding. A half hour later on this March morning in 1979, ski train No. 11, at left on the facing page, visits Crescent. The consist includes two *Zephyr* dome cars for the mayor of Denver's annual ski party to Winter Park.

R.L.

R.L.

R.L.

D&RGW No. 15, i.e. Amtrak No. 5

In 1971, under the assumption that Rio Grande was going to join the National Railroad Passenger Corporation, Amtrak assumed its Chicago-San Francisco train would operate via D&RGW. Rio Grande rebuffed NRPC and the rest is history. Ironically, the Amtrak train in question carried the name *California Zephyr* from May to November 1971 when it was renamed *San Francisco Zephyr*. The photo above carries the irony a bit further: A derailment on rival Union Pacific at Green River, Wyoming, in April 1978 resulted in the Amtrak train being detoured over Rio Grande between Denver and Salt Lake City. The westbound detour SFZ backed into Denver Union Station just as the CZ had done for years, and at 1 p.m. (nearly assuming the schedule of the long-defunct *Exposition Flyer*) found itself on D&RGW rails operating as D&RGW train 15. At 2 p.m. it rolled through Crescent.

at twenty-nine

Tunnel 29 just east of Pinecliffe was a popular location for photographers in pursuit of No. 17. On the facing page, F9 5771 emerges from the ultra-short bore, and at right the cliffs above South Boulder Creek afford an overall view of Tunnel 29. Below, a track inspector and his motorcar wait in the siding at Pinecliffe for No. 17 to clear.

Pinecliffe sidestep

Bridge freight traffic was brisk on the D&RGW throughout the 1970s, but this didn't prevent the road from treating the *Zephyr* as its premier train. At Cliff siding in May 1979, a freight from Salt Lake City with a 1962-vintage GP30 on the point steps aside for the No. 17. On the facing page, the engineer notches up the 567's near Rollinsville during the train's westbound climb on Thanksgiving day 1978.

M.P.

R.L.

Between Cliff and Rollinsville the railroad saddles up to South Boulder Creek and penetrates a short, rocky canyon to reach the wide valley floor [or park in Colorado parlance] leading to Moffat Tunnel. The hillside and trackside views on this page show No. 17 snaking through the canyon. Rollinsville was a busy stage stop before the coming of the railroad, but now it's just a small watering hole for skiers, campers, and the occasional photographer.

R.L.

R.L.

the Divide
and its conqueror

Snowstorms are measured in dollars instead of inches by the Colorado ski industry, but for *Rio Grande Zephyr* patrons snow is measured in sensory pleasure, for under no other circumstances is the cozy warmth aboard a train more permeating than during a whirling mountain blizzard. Here the westbound *Zephyr* drifts through the S curves near East Portal in a swirl of white before ducking into the quiet blackness of Moffat Tunnel.

R.L.

During the summer months, the eastbound *Rio Grande Zephyr* rambled through the high valley east of Moffat Tunnel in the dwindling rays of sunlight. No. 18 is on the tangent east of Rollinsville at 7:35 p.m. in June 1975.

2

Grande River

ORIGINALLY NAMED Grand River during the nineteenth century, the Colorado River provides the present D&RGW with a relatively direct route west through the myriad of mountain ranges of western Colorado. The Zephyr route along the river includes segments of several ancestral railroads: the Denver, Northwestern & Pacific, which followed the river from Granby to Orestod; the Denver & Salt Lake Western, which built the Dotsero Cutoff; the original narrow gauge Denver & Rio Grande main line out of Pueblo through Glenwood Canyon; and the Rio Grande Junction Railway, which operated the joint trackage for the Rio Grande and Colorado Midland from Newcastle to Grand Junction. The final piece to the trackage jigsaw puzzle was put in place when the D&RGW relocated a portion of its main line west of Glenwood Springs on original CM alignment.

In contrast to the roar of the Zephyr's EMD 567 engines on the ascent from the plains to the summit deep within Moffat Tunnel, No. 17's tour through the Colorado River portion of its route was characterized by quiet tempo as the train rolled downgrade for over 230 miles from Granby to the Utah state line. For certain, there were straightaways on which the Zephyr could make a Notch Eight sprint; moreover, the train's customary leisurely pace through numerous canyons enhanced the apparent speed on those brief tangents in Middle Park or Grand Valley.

Glenwood Springs, the semi-fashionable resort at the west end of magical Glenwood Canyon, was the focal point of the trip along the Colorado. Like the California Zephyr decades, passenger loadings for Glenwood throughout the 1970s necessitated extra cars on weekend Zephyr trips. As the primary destination for most Zephyr patrons, Glenwood at train time was almost incongruous in the age of vans, Winnebagos, and the camper-toting family station wagon. But Zephyr clientele were not the stereotyped poor who had no other choice but to ride. To the contrary, the charisma of the Rio Grande Zephyr encompassed the mystique of stylish trains of years begone. You could see it in the affluent, leisure-oriented tourists of the 1970s crowding aboard No. 18, beating a path to Silver Sky for an enduring social scene during the evening trip back to Denver. For Coloradoans, the Rio Grande Zephyr was an unparalleled way to make a weekend getaway to the mountains.

Westbound the *Zephyr* traversed the valley and canyon of the Fraser River before settling down to the 238-mile run along the Colorado River. Below, the Continental Divide becomes a majestic backdrop for No. 18 sweeping through the upland valley of the Fraser. By the time No. 17 arrived at Granby (facing page, top left), breakfast had been served and steward George Brooks and his crew relax at the temporarily vacant tables of *Silver Banquet*. The magnificent scenery which drew so many riders to the *Zephyr* was just a blur of another trip for the veteran dining-car crew.

R.L.

R.L.

R.L.

M.P.

out to lunch

Of the numerous watercourses probed by the RGZ and predecessor CZ for more than 30 years, few were more publicized than Byers just west of Hot Sulphur Springs. Two transcontinental pathways share the short canyon on opposite sides of the Colorado River: D&RGW and highway U.S. 40. Above, a seven-car No. 17 rambles through Byers at 20 mph in 1974.

following pages

The westbound *Zephyr* prowls into precipitous Gore Canyon west of Kremmling, and on the companion page slices through an adjacent chasm just east of Radium, known as Black Gorge on U.S. Geological Survey maps and Little Gore on the D&RGW. Usually only a couple of fishermen or adventure-seeking rafters witness the passing of trains through the canyons west of Kremmling.   R.L. M.P.

serpentine
scenario

Between Kremmling and Bond, the *Zephyr's* second scheduled stop, the railroad route slips away from numbered highways to explore remote valleys, gorges, and near-ghost towns. Yarmony, Radium, and State Bridge are the only signs of civilization and these settlements are but three or four buildings each. In this four-photo sequence, No. 17 coasts downgrade through the curves east of Radium.

R.L.

R.L.

R.L.

Alice Loveman

R.L.

Alice Loveman

rails through Radium

On the facing page, a six-car No. 17 with a GP30 on the point rolls through the valley at Radium siding in September 1974 while above, No. 18 glides through the hamlet in April of that same year. The Colorado's valley east of Gore is one of idyllic scenery, and most *Zephyr* patrons continued to opt for dome amenities on this portion of the trip. However, a few forsook the scenery (temporarily at least) to sit downstairs and chat with new friends or to sit alone and catch up on writing old friends.

During the decade of the 1970s, exploding demands for coal fulfilled Dave Moffat's dream of tapping the region's resources, and an ever-increasing parade of coal trains rolled from the Craig branch onto the main line at Orestod. It was not uncommon for the *Zephyr* to meet Moffat Extras during its morning ramble down the Western Slope. On the facing page and at left, No. 17 meets an eastbound coal train at the west switch of Yarmony siding. Below, Webster's definition of anachronism—any inconsistency in the matter of time—is brought to life at State Bridge in March 1979 as the CZ 30th Anniversary version of the *Rio Grande Zephyr* approaches the rustic settlement.

following pages

Celebration versions of the *Rio Grande Zephyr* weren't limited to CZ anniversaries. The panorama that follows depicts the special Moffat Tunnel 50th Anniversary consist of the *Rio Grande Zephyr* coiling through State Bridge in February 1978. The ancient wooden bridge spanning the Colorado predates train and trees as well as Moffat Tunnel itself.

R.L.

R.L.

R.L.

It's high noon and No. 18 is rolling down the Dotsero Cutoff near Burns at a steady 40 mph. Motorists on the highway overpass at Dotsero rarely notice the plaque identifying the corporate background involved in the construction of the trackage beneath.

following pages

The westbound *Zephyr*, with a GP40 subbing for the F9A 5771, sweeps through the horseshoe curve at Dell siding, a third of the way down the Cutoff.

M.P.

M.P.

M.P.

California Zephyr brochures of years past often featured views of Glenwood Canyon's lofty walls to typify the scenery along the CZ route, but the two photos on this page select track-level scenes of the *Rio Grande Zephyr* in the canyon. Above, vestibule riders savor the mountain air from the rear door of a Shriners reserved car. At left, evergreens frame No. 17 as it slows for Glenwood Springs.

The *California Zephyr* 25th Anniversary version of No. 18, facing page, advances upgrade along the silvery currents of the Colorado River moments after departing Glenwood Springs. The consist included every stainless-steel car on the Rio Grande roster: four dome coaches, the dome coffee shop, two flat-top coaches, the diner, and the dome observation-lounge. In March 1974, few trains could compare to No. 18 on this day.

M.P.

M.P.

R.L.

Glenwood holiday

There were, of course, hundreds of stations in the U. S. still served by passenger trains during the 1970s, but the stone-and-brick depot at Glenwood Springs had to qualify as one of the most picturesque. Aside from Denver, Glenwood was also the busiest depot on the *Zephyr* route in terms of passenger loadings. It was not at all unusual for a hundred or more passengers to detrain from a Saturday *Zephyr* and disperse to the region's numerous hotels and resorts for a weekend retreat. The almost painting-like tableau of passengers waiting for No. 18 in the classic scene on the facing page certainly is a happy indication that some things never really change: Except for dress, the row of passengers anticipating an approaching train is Americana at its best, and it could have been Anyplace U.S.A. at anytime in history since passenger trains began stopping at stations. Norman Rockwell would be pleased.

R.L.

M.P.

R.L.

R.L.

R.L.

R.L.

R.L.

At far left on the facing page, No. 17, with bell ringing, is about to pull to a stop under the Colorado 82 highway bridge just west of Glenwood Springs depot. The *Zephyr's* 10-minute pause at the resort hub was an Event, and as these scenes depict, people showed up at train time for diverse reasons. Some met arriving loved ones or posed for a family portrait in front of the famous *Zephyr*. Some were local folk who just strolled down to the station and sat on the benches under the old trees or rested on the lawn and discussed the day's events with the *Zephyr* engineer.

At left, a girl scout troup relishes the anticipation of a train ride to Grand Junction as they stand ready to board No. 17. At far right on this page, resort limousines meet the *Zephyr*, picking up guests at trainside.

R.L.

R.L.

63

Glenwood
good-byes

All too soon the last passenger steps aboard and the baggageman wheels his cargo into the station building: departure time is imminent. Shortly, the conductor makes his "Board!" call, diesels rev, and *Silver Sky* slips past the platforms signifying that the Event has ended for another day.

seventy along Seventy

Beyond Glenwood, No. 17 sprints west across the Grand Valley, and picture-taking from the vestibule becomes a little difficult as the *Zephyr* train overtakes motorists on parallel Interstate 70 at 70 mph. Below right, the train momentarily diverges from the highway alignment as it curves under the Newcastle underpass.

R.L.

R.L.

R.L.

After lunch, a couple of passengers who have probably seen the scenery several times before opt for a game of backgammon in *Silver Banquet*, as the train rolls obediently through the tangents east of Silt.

shotgun approach

With a name like Rifle, one would almost expect a log-cabin depot with cowboys on horses greeting the train, but a modern frame depot (facing page) with passengers chauffered in by Chevys is more the norm. Don't be mislead by the trickle of passengers about to board No. 18: Throughout the 1970s the Rio Grande ran a well-maintained, refurbished *Zephyr*, and despite lack of advertising, patronage increased respectfully during the decade. The train was its own advertisement. An ad agency couldn't have said it better.

fast freights in waiting

The Zephyr always promenaded past a parade of Denver- and Pueblo-bound freights tucked into numerous sidings along the Grand Valley between Glenwood Springs and Grand Junction. At right an eastbound freight is already beginning to roll from the east end of Una siding as No. 17 approaches the west turnout. Below, No. 17 passes the head end of an eastbound at Akin in Debeque Canyon; below right, the dome observation-lounge flies by another freight on the fast track to Grand Junction.

M.P.

R.L.

M.P.

A meet between two passenger trains was a rare occurrence on the Rio Grande of the 1970s. In October 1974, the railroad ran a westbound inspection train for officials and so provided an opportunity for this passenger train - meets - passenger train scene. No. 18 has dutifully entered Clifton siding just east of Grand Junction to let the classy special by, the consist of which includes a brand-new SD40T-2, GP40, steam-generator unit, borrowed UP sleeper, dome coach, diner *Silver Banquet,* and business car 100 *Wilson McCarthy.* No. 18 carries a typical consist, but with dome coffee shop *Silver Shop* subbing for *Silver Banquet.*

M.P.

R.L.

M.P.

a pause
that refreshes

Grand Junction evokes visions of Colorado Midland trains arriving and departing with another generation of travelers. Indeed, the depot itself—dating from 1905—remains virtually unchanged from those halcyon days of Colorado railroading. But as far as steel-wheeled conveyances are concerned, only the *Rio Grande Zephyr* continued the tradition of service to Denver and Salt Lake City. Above, No. 18 poses proudly beside the stately building. Inside, the agent tends to last-minute sales while the conductor clears his bookkeeping at the check-in table and sends another family off to the waiting *Zephyr*.

R.L.

While regular passengers climb aboard and depot personnel complete their predeparture duties, the baggageman loads bikes into the combine as a bicycling fraternity opts for the *Zephyr's* wheels back to Denver. Although the D&RGW commissary at Denver stocked the dining and lounge facilities, Grand Junction is the focal point for routine train servicing: Both east and westbound *Zephyrs* were fueled and watered here for the Grand Junction-Denver and Grand Junction-Salt Lake round trips.

R.L.

M.P.

R.L.

M.P.

Grand Junction is virtually the midway point for the RGZ's 570-mile one-way trip, and the second of three crew-change locations west from Denver. Both train and engine crews changed here. Above, a Utah Division engineer climbs aboard for the three-hour journey to Helper, Utah.

never on Wednesday

THERE WAS a time when most railroads' premier streamliners were entities, fixed sets of equipment dedicated to specific routes. There's a host of examples: Union Pacific's original *City* trains, Central of Georgia's Budd-built *Man O' War*, Great Northern's incomparable *Empire Builder*, et al. Unfortunately, economics and efficiency triumphed over aesthetics, forcing railroads and, later, Amtrak as well to conduct passenger train operations from a pool of equipment and locomotives.

But that contemporary practice did not apply to a 1970s D&RGW whose modest passenger car roster protected but a single train: the *Rio Grande Zephyr*. So there it was, a surviving example of an individualized streamliner. That's right; there was but one set of locomotives and equipment assigned to Nos. 17 and 18. Oh, passenger-load fluctuations dictated consists of varying length throughout the decade, and mechanical ailments for the 1955-vintage F units resulted in substitute power on occasion, but the essence of the RGZ operation was the predictable nature of its consist, schedule, and patrons—much like its *California Zephyr* ancestor.

Just by noting variations in its consist you could see that the RGZ was principally a tourist operation catering to the Denver populace. No. 17 often would depart Denver Union Terminal on Saturday mornings with a full consist of nine cars as young and old populated weekend *Zephyr* runs. Weekday departures were usually shorter: five cars in winter, eight cars during the summer .

Burnham Shops in Denver was home for the nine Budd-built ex-*California Zephyr* cars and two Pullman-Standard ex-*Prospector* combines, and also the base for all maintenance, cleaning, and repair work on the rolling stock. So, what went out on No. 17 one day came back the next on No. 18. Except for Wednesday, of course—that was the *Zephyr*'s day off, a day spent typically by the Burnham Shop crews reconditioning the train for another week of galloping 3420 miles back and forth across the American West.

power for the people

By 1973 D&RGW possessed only three EMD F units, assigned solely to the *Zephyr*. To be sure, each F experienced its share of mechanical breakdowns throughout the decade, but the railroad always hastened to put a delinquent unit back on the road as quickly as possible. Freight units (usually GP30's, GP35's, or GP40's) dispatched to rescue or substitute ailing *Zephyr* power may have dampened the aesthetics of the regal train appearancewise, but more importantly passengers were delivered to their promised destinations. F9A 5771 clad in D&RGW's splendid Aspen gold and silver, above, is the "Queen of the Fleet." It is estimated that by the close of the 1970s the 1955-born 5771 had logged nearly 3 million miles, mostly in *Zephyr* service.

R.L.

R.L.

F9B twin sisters 5762 and 5763 are shown as they appeared in March 1979. The 5762 had been rebuilt in 1978 with a new prime mover, new metal-faced sheathing, and a fresh coat of paint. The grimy, rusted-out carbody of sister 5763 was more indicative of the toil the F's had faced in more than two decades of service; for her rebuild would come late in 1979. Steam generator 253, below, was used from November to May to assist in keeping passengers warm and cozy. Rio Grande converted two Alco PB passenger units (originally part of two Alco passenger diesel sets Rio Grande purchased for CZ service in 1947) into non-powered steam-generator vehicles 252 and 253. In addition, the roster included steam generators 250 and 251, built from steam locomotive tenders. The 250 was stationed at Salt Lake City to protect the *Zephyr*, and 251 was used exclusively on the ski train.

R.L.

Rio Grande acquired Pullman-Standard combines 1230 and 1231 in 1950 when it re-equipped the *Prospector*, and they were the only *Prospector* cars retained on the roster after the Denver-Salt Lake City overnighter was discontinued in May 1967. During the early years of RGZ operation, one of the combines was repainted silver to better blend with the Budd-built *Zephyr* cars, but in 1975 it was put back into Aspen gold which adhered to metal sheathing better. The combines served a threefold purpose: baggage car, conductor's office, and passenger overflow car.

it's pleasant under glass

In 1948 Budd Company of Philadelphia built 18 dome coaches for *California Zephyr* service. CB&Q and WP owned seven each and D&RGW, four. Domes were the fundamental—if not essential—element of the CZ, and after the train's premature death in 1970, Grande's four dome coaches indeed became the fundamental element of *Rio Grande Zephyr* service. At times all four cars, minus CZ nameboards but still sporting their original car names and CZ line numbers, were pressed into duty to accommodate the growing number of riders. When light patronage was anticipated, one or two of the domes could be rotated out of the consist and into Burnham Shops at Denver for maintenance, reserving Wednesdays express-ly for working on the diner or dome obser-vation-lounge, the two cars that had to be on duty six days a week. Dome coach interiors [top right, facing page] retained their classic Budd look, although in some the carpeting had been removed. Often a whole car would be assigned to a special group such as scouts or church societies and literally become a clubhouse on wheels.

Silver Pony

R.L.

Silver Mustang

R.L.

Silver Bronco

R.L.

Silver Colt

R.L.

"As you travel over this bountiful land of ours, may you be ever reminded of the grace Almighty God has bestowed upon us. Let us acknowledge our debt to Him with prayers of thanksgiving."

Rio Grande Zephyr Grill
Luncheon Selections

TO INSURE PROMPT SERVICE PLEASE WRITE EACH ITEM ON MEAL CHECK

Tomato Juice	.40	Grapefruit Juice	.40

Individual Soups:
Chicken, Mushroom, Tomato, Vegetable, Clam Chowder .... .60

SUGGESTIONS

Filet of Fresh Fish	2.25
Grilled Salisbury Steak	2.20
Minced Ham Omelette	1.95

Potato, Vegetable, Bread and Butter, Coffee, Tea or Milk served with above orders

SANDWICHES

Hamburger	1.45
Ham	1.20
Ham and Cheese	1.45
Bacon, Lettuce and Tomato	1.45
Sardine, Domestic	1.40
Toasted Cheese	1.10

Served plain or on toast

Lettuce and Tomato Salad, Club Dressing 1.00

Toast or Crackers

Pie	.60	Ice Cream	.40
Peaches in Syrup	.50	Pears in Syrup	.50
Coffee, Cup	.30	Decaffeinated Coffee, Cup	.30
Tea, Cup	.30	Milk, Half Pint	.30

Hot Chocolate, Cup .30

Parents may share their portions with children without extra charge or half portions will be served to children under 12 years of age at half meal cost.

COMPLETE BEVERAGE LIST AVAILABLE
In Lounge Car
Additional charge will be made for service outside of the Grill Car.
This service is subject to delay when Grill Car is busy.
L. J. Bernstein, Director-Passenger and Dining Car Services
Denver & Rio Grande Western Railroad, Denver, Colorado 80217

Rio Grande
the ACTION road

6/74-200

"As you travel over this bountiful land of ours, may you be ever reminded of the grace Almighty God has bestowed upon us. Let us acknowledge our debt to Him with prayers of thanksgiving."

Rio Grande Zephyr Grill
Dinner Selections

TO INSURE PROMPT SERVICE PLEASE WRITE EACH ITEM ON MEAL CHECK

Tomato Juice	.40	Grapefruit Juice	.40
		Soup du Jour, Cup	.55

SUGGESTIONS

Tomato Juice		Soup du Jour	
Grilled Native Mountain Trout (10 oz.)			3.65
Ham Steak Saute, with Eggs			3.25
Grilled Choice Club Steak (8 oz.)			4.25

Potato		Vegetable	
Coffee	Tea	Milk	Decaffeinated Coffee
Assorted Pies	Ice Cream	Peaches in Syrup

SANDWICHES

Hamburger	1.45
Bacon, Lettuce and Tomato	1.45
Grilled Ham	1.20
Ham and Cheese	1.45
Sardine, Domestic	1.40
Toasted Cheese	1.10

Served plain or on toast

Lettuce and Tomato Salad, Club Dressing 1.00

Toast or Crackers

Pie	.60	Ice Cream	.40
Peaches in Syrup	.50	Pears in Syrup	.50
Coffee, Cup	.30	Decaffeinated Coffee, Cup	.30
Tea, Cup	.30	Milk, Half Pint	.30

Hot Chocolate, Cup .30

Parents may share their portions with children without extra charge or half portions, excepting Mountain Trout or Steak, will be served to children under 12 years of age at half menu price.

COMPLETE BEVERAGE LIST AVAILABLE
In Lounge Car
Additional charge will be made for service outside of the Grill Car.
This service is subject to delay when Grill Car is busy.
L. J. Bernstein, Director-Passenger and Dining Car Services
Denver & Rio Grande Western Railroad, Denver, Colorado 80217

Rio Grande
the ACTION road

6/74-200

M.P.

Good Morning

"As you travel over this bountiful land of ours, may you be ever reminded of the grace Almighty God has bestowed upon us. Let us acknowledge our debt to Him with prayers of thanksgiving."

Rio Grande Zephyr Grill

Breakfast Menu

TO INSURE PROMPT SERVICE PLEASE WRITE EACH ITEM ON MEAL CHECK

Orange Juice	.40	Tomato Juice	.40
Grapefruit Juice	.40	Half Grapefruit	.55
	Breakfast Prunes	.55	

All Bran	.55	Bran Flakes	.55
Corn Flakes	.55	Special K	.55
	Rolled Oats	.55	

Cereals served with choice of milk or half and half

Bacon or Ham with Eggs and Toast	2.00
Griddle Cakes .90, With Bacon or Ham	1.55
Two Eggs, Boiled, Fried or Scrambled and Toast	1.10

Coffee, Tea or Milk included with above

Sweet Roll .30

Dry or Buttered Toast with Jelly .30

Coffee, Cup	.30	Orange Pekoe Tea, Cup	.30
Milk, Half Pint	.30	Decaffeinated Coffee, Cup	.30

Hot Chocolate, Cup .30

Additional charge will be made for service outside the Grill Car.
This service is subject to delay when Grill Car is busy.
L. J. Bernstein, Director-Passenger and Dining Car Services
Denver & Rio Grande Western Railroad, Denver, Colorado 80217

Rio Grande
the ACTION road

6/74-200

Rio Grande Zephyr Grill (Silver Shop) menus from June 1974, courtesy D&RGW. Prices subject to change.

78

R.L.

Silver Shop

R.L.

a stand-in . . .

Silver Shop, facing page, is an ex-CZ dome buffet-lounge-dormitory [to CZ patrons, the Cable Car Lounge] which in *Rio Grande Zephyr* service became a protection car for the diner and dome observation-lounge. The view at Grand Junction shows *Silver Shop* substituting for diner *Silver Banquet*, while below it kicks up snow while pinch-hitting for observation-lounge *Silver Sky*. Because of *Shop*'s small galley, menus had to be of a more-limited scope when it was used as a diner, and as a lounge it lacked some of the amenities and capacity of *Silver Sky*. Nonetheless, *Shop*'s importance is duly noted because it permitted D&RGW to maintain a reliable *Zephyr* service and fulfill the public timetable commitment to lounge and dining service.

M.P.

Silver Aspen

R.L.

Silver Pine

R.L.

and sit downs

As passenger loadings increased during the middle years of the 1970s, so did the railroad's dependence on its two unusual flat-top coaches, *Silver Pine* and *Silver Aspen*. These two cars and four sister cars (for WP and CB&Q) were built in 1948 as 16-section sleepers for the CZ and rebuilt to coaches in the 1960s. Until 1976 the flat-tops usually ran behind the dome coaches, but after that time they were positioned between combine and domes. Above is an interior view of one of the 44-seat coaches.

Silver Banquet

R.L.

as you travel over this bountiful land . . .

Breakfast, lunch, and dinner was a treasured experience for travelers in the dining room of *Silver Banquet* on the *Rio Grande Zephyr.* RGZ menus offered few gourmet dining possibilities, but the quality and portions of entries were incomparable to most other rolling restaurants in the U.S. In spite of a couple of galley fires that occurred during the 1970s, *Silver Banquet* provided satisfying meals for Zephyr patrons into the 1980s although D&RGW in 1979 purchased a former UP diner to use as a backup for *Banquet.*

M.P.

M.P.

M.P.

lounge in the Sky

By 1980 *Silver Sky* was one of the few operating survivors of a remarkable passenger car design and styling instigated by Budd in 1947 with the inauguration of dome observation-parlor cars on Burlington's *Twin Cities Zephyrs*. *Silver Sky* was one of six dome sleeper-observation-lounge cars built in 1948 for the CZ, and in 1971 it became the mainstay for RGZ lounge service. Whereas RGZ coaches could be rotated in and out of the consist as needs and servicing demanded, *Silver Sky* was scheduled to operate on every trip. By the end of the decade the wear and grime associated with such intense service was beginning to show, but dirt and dents notwithstanding, the handsome car visibly punctuated the tail end of the *Zephyr* in a style of service of years past.

M.P.

Silver Sky

SILVER SKY

R.L.

a feast and a toast

If dome cars provided a rail-born amenity that had become increasingly rare by the close of the 1970s, then surely the last two cars of the *Rio Grande Zephyr* provided a combination that was virtually unique in American train travel in 1979. Below, No. 17 races by Desert Switch, Utah, with *Silver Banquet* and *Silver Sky* bringing up the markers in Grande style.

M.P.

4

wild West

IF THE Colorado River simply flowed west to Salt Lake City, the remainder of the *Zephyr's* trip probably would have been much like that between Glenwood Springs and the Utah state line: a gentle downgrade journey along the meandering river in its wide, cliff-lined valley. But the Colorado doesn't do that, of course. At the Utah-Colorado border the river parts company with railroad at the west end of enchanting Ruby Canyon and angles south toward Arizona. Ruby Canyon is the *Zephyr's* gateway into Utah, and once inside the Mormon State, D&RGW rails climb away from the watercourse and introduce the *Zephyr* to still another chapter of the American West: the upland desert.

Once again the tempo of the trip transforms. Now it's a 70 mph, 138-mile trip across a baked-hard desert to Helper, at the eastern foot of the Wasatch Mountains. The high desert is a unique section of the *Zephyr* route. The horizon-to-horizon flatness that usually dominates a tourist's preconception of a desert is quickly altered by the moonlike features of the Book Cliffs which loom immediately to the north of the Rio Grande main line. In all other respects, classic desert it is: barren gulley washes, scrub vegetation, and pastels of orange, brown, and yellow. It is a region where one can fully comtemplate the pure expanse of the American West or the endless aeons of time in its making.

Most of the minor settlements in the desert region are virtual ghost towns from the days before CTC and interstate highways. Consequently, passenger loadings at the station stops between Grand Junction and Helper/Price—Thompson and Green River—were almost nonexistent. A couple of times a week, perhaps, the *Zephyr* paused at the Thompson flagstop to deliver a passenger whose relatives resided at nearby Moab or take on a footweary backpacker from the Arches National Monument south of town.

If ever there was a vehicle that truly enhanced its environment, surely it was the *Rio Grande Zephyr*. The *Zephyr* spent 88 hours a week on the road, and for approximately 18 of those hours every week, the *Zephyr* added to the natural beauty of eastern Utah. Should the *Zephyr* species ever become extinct, so shall a part of the serene beauty that is the upland desert.

M.P.

remarkable Ruby Canyon

Ruby Canyon straddles the Utah-Colorado border and is a transition zone between the irrigated Grand Valley to the east and desolate desert country to the west. Passengers aboard the *Rio Grande Zephyr*, here slicing along the tangent east of Utaline siding, didn't have to worry about buffalo stampedes or Indian attacks, but this *is* an inhospitable land. If the sizzling sun and the alkaline earth aren't enough to keep strangers out of the area, ranchers' warning signs probably will.

M.P.

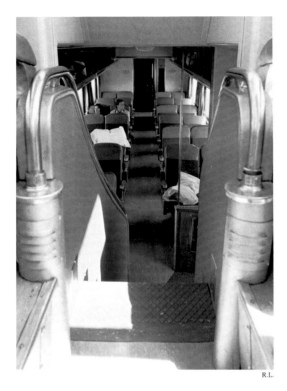

R.L.

The above view from the top of the dome steps gives evidence of the sparse passenger loadings west of Grand Junction. At right, a six-car consist typical of the mid-1970s sweeps through the middle of Ruby Canyon bathed in late afternoon sunlight.

M.P.

It's cocktail time in *Silver Sky* as the westbound *Zephyr*, facing page, cruises along the eroded sandstone cliffs of Ruby Canyon. Although Gore Canyon is the most awesome defile along the *Zephyr* route, riders are usually more entranced by the vivid colors of remote Ruby Canyon. It is in this watercourse that the Colorado really begins to reveal its sculpting powers, which reach their zenith at the incredible Grand Canyon hundreds of miles downstream.

Even the presence of railroad officials traveling in office car *Wilson McCarthy* could not forestall an occasional operating problem. On this wintry day in March 1979 the 5771's brakes had locked as the eastbound *Zephyr* made its station stop at Thompson. Although the brakes eventually released, No. 18 had to travel at a much reduced speed because of severe flat spots on the wheels. By the time the photo at right was recorded at Whitehouse, Utah Division Superintendent Larry Parsons, riding in the cab, had called the dispatcher to have a local section crew meet the train at Cisco with their rail grinding equipment in hopes of making quick repair to the wheels. The saga continues on the following two pages.

M.P.

one of those days

When the *Zephyr* limped into Cisco, the section crew was already stationed at the east switch. After a futile attempt to grind out the flat spots, Superintendent Parsons concluded that the best solution was to subtract the problem: cut 5771 from the train and replace it with a unit pilfered from the next passing freight.

M.P.

A westbound freight due by within the hour was contacted, and eventually it nosed up to the east end of Cisco siding to begin rescue maneuvers. Crews tacked an eastward-facing GP40 from the freight's locomotive consist onto the *Zephyr*'s FB's and shunted ailing F9A 5771 onto the house track. Finally, the reassembled freight moved on and a three-hour-late *Zephyr* resumed its journey to Grand Junction and points east. And that's the saga at Cisco, kids.

Between Grand Junction and Helper, the speed limit tops at 70 for freight and passenger trains alike. Here No. 18 brakes for a 55 mph restrictive curve near Whitehouse siding.

With few passengers to tend to on the west end of the Zephyr route, the trainman has plenty of time to discuss the railroad and its scenery with a couple of elderly women who have opted to avoid the late afternoon sun in the dome. Below, the Zephyr tops a grade on a fill just east of Thompson as it approaches the desert outpost.

R.L.

M.P.

M.P.

R.L.

train time at Thompson

Thompson is a speck of an oasis on the desert plateau. Until
the Interstate highway was completed south of town in
1976, all highway traffic rumbled through the near-ghost
town and past the well-maintained, flat-roofed depot. The
depot's living quarters also served as home for agent Jim
O'Neil who, aside from selling tickets to Grand Junction,
Denver and the like, also kept record of the day's high and
low temperatures for the U.S. Weather Bureau.

M.P.

R.L.

M.P.

The uninhabited desert begins where Thompson depot platform ends. In the sequence across the top of these two pages, the *Zephyr* rolls off the desert for a brief pause at the isolated flagstop. With Thompson passengers entrained, the conductor, above, highballs the engineer while the train attendant wonders about the canine's travel plans. At right, No. 18 sweeps through the reverse curves east of the depot moments after departure.

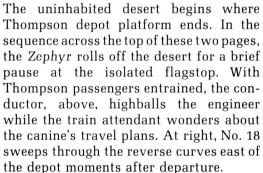

For those who were along for the *Zephyr* ride west of Grand Junction, the run beside Book Cliffs was a remarkable train-riding experience in an untamed (visually at least) West. On the following pages a seven-car Vista-Dome No. 18 skims through Brendel on a Sunday morning in 1975.   M.P.

R.L.

The land surrounding remote Green River, the geographical low point on the Denver–Salt Lake route, is virtually without life and free of honky-tonk roadside establishments, garish signs, and, save for the constant, businesslike passage of freight trains, other signs of man's omnipresence. On these two pages we see the *Zephyr* on its high-speed journey through this desert: at right, thundering past intermediate signals east of Solitude; below, meeting the *Ford Fast Train* at Desert; and in the almost surrealistic scene on the facing page, skirting the base of the Book Cliffs near Floy.

R.L.

M.P.

M.P.

desert tracks

Continual track maintenance is a must under the extreme weather conditions endured on the desert plateau. Above, moments after No. 18's passage, a track gang resumes work at Woodside siding as a spring rainstorm approaches from the south. Below, a nine-car *Zephyr* revels in brilliant sunshine as it approaches the restrictive curves near Grassy, while on the facing page an isolated five-car train recedes under ominous skies down the endless tangents west of Solitude, east of forever.

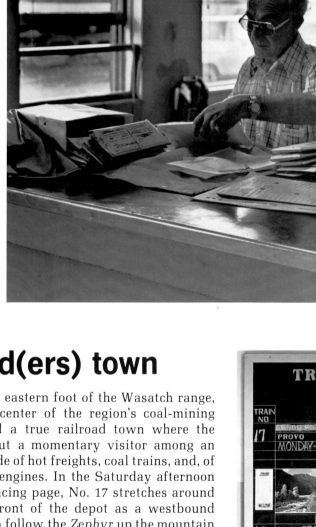

railroad(ers) town

Situated at the eastern foot of the Wasatch range, Helper is the center of the region's coal-mining operations and a true railroad town where the *Zephyr* was but a momentary visitor among an incessant parade of hot freights, coal trains, and, of course, helper engines. In the Saturday afternoon scene on the facing page, No. 17 stretches around the curve in front of the depot as a westbound freight waits to follow the *Zephyr* up the mountain and beyond to Salt Lake City. Inside the depot, agents burrow through their round-the-clock duties of marshalling waybills, crews, and trains in and out of town.

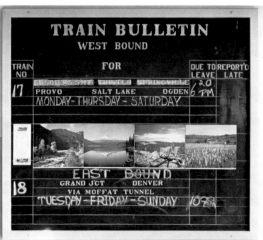

M.P.

R.L.

R.L.

R.L.

Like several other intermediate stops along the *Zephyr* route, Helper generated little passenger business. It was a service stop, and it was the railroaders who attended to the mechanical needs of trains and locomotives that gave Helper its character. Each day when No. 18 arrived from Provo, crews inspected running gear and washed 5771's windshield. At bottom right on the facing page, venerable 5771 leads a five-car No. 18 past another old-timer, SD9 5300 waiting opposite the Helper depot. At right, the relief engineer climbs aboard the vintage cab unit to resume No. 18's sojourn across the desert.

Sandstone cliffs reflect the evening lights of Helper like crumpled foil as No. 17 amid veils of steam vapor glistens from the station platform lights. Passengers on board settle down to Baked Rocky Mountain Trout in *Silver Banquet* or sip Sloe Gin Fizz's in *Silver Sky*, far removed from the ice-encrusted environment outside. Ahead: a march up Soldier Summit.

5
military mountain

AFTER the race across the high desert, No. 17 deserved a rest. And got it, at Helper. Here the *Rio Grande Zephyr* paused for 10 minutes to catch its breath and change crews. Like wrestlers between rounds, the locomotives were quickly and efficiently tended to by service crews. Windshields were wiped clean and running gear inspected. And then, with bell ringing, the *Zephyr* eased west from the depot for the final round: the climb to Soldier Summit. Watch out, Wasatch! Matters were less strenuous in *Silver Banquet*, where fresh linens and place settings of sparkling china and silverware beckoned dinner guests. Roast Lamb and Rio Grande Chef's Salad awaited those who would, from their ringside seats in the diner, watch the grades of the Price River Canyon fall away into twilight.

Once clear of the summit, No. 17 descended through Spanish Fork Canyon and made a final sprint through the Salt Lake Valley night. Passengers knew they had returned to civilization—the muffled bamps of 5771's air horns told them that as the *Zephyr* bounded across the numerous grade crossings of Provo and a string of other communities. And now the day's visits and exaltations rapidly became memory, and remaining passengers sensed a common unity as they were left to contemplate the future of the cinderella train.

The *Zephyr's* arrival at Salt Lake City was without fanfare. The brick-and-stone depot was nearly deserted, and often the *Zephyr* crew outnumbered passengers. The limousine service to Ogden for connection with Amtrak to the west was only moderately more inconvenient than the across-the-platform SP connection that existed at that city prior to Amtrak day 1971, when the short-lived "California Service" version of the RGZ operated through to Ogden. During the last years of the 1970s, RGZ passengers also had the option of walking two blocks to UP's Salt Lake station for new Amtrak connections to Seattle and Los Angeles. For the RGZ engine, lounge, and dining car crew, though, there was only the bus connection uptown for the hotel and a short night's rest before going on duty the next morning to return the *Rio Grande Zephyr* to life as train No. 18.

Domes are good places to be during the climb over Soldier Summit. This double-track saddle of the Wasatch Mountains sees 20 or more trains daily, and often, through the agency of reverse-signaled CTC, the *Zephyr* was routed around struggling freights. At Utah Railway Junction, below, the eastbound *Zephyr* obeys the instructions of CTC signals and gracefully snakes from the westbound track to eastbound iron. Utah Railway trains are channeled onto the D&RGW at the junction and have trackage rights west to Thistle.

M.P.

M.P.

C.T.C. in action

Below, the dispatcher in Denver some 455 rail miles away has No. 17 on the eastward track as it grinds upgrade near Utah Junction. At right, the famous Castle Gate rock formation dwarfs the eastbound *Zephyr* easing down the westbound main on a 2.4 per cent grade.

M.P.

R.L.

M.P.

M.P.

a glimmer of hope

With the early months of 1979 came an increase in "Zephyr Awareness" by the media and residents of the Salt Lake Valley. The cause: D&RGW's petition to discontinue the Zephyr west of Grand Junction. On the facing page, No. 18 rolls downgrade through the reverse curves of the upper Price River Canyon while inside Silver Sky a Salt Lake City TV crew tapes an interview with the conductor (above). As the Zephyr rolled on and the months wore by, senior cook Tex Jones often would savor the vestibule views of the canyons that had been a part of his life for so many years. Fortunately for Tex and thousands of passengers, the Interstate Commerce Commission on the afternoon of March 31, 1979, postponed the Zephyr cutback for one more year.

M.P.

Above left, approaching Gilluly on the west side of the pass, No. 18 breaks the chilly solitude of a bright winter day. As the eastbound train loops around the lower of the Gilluly loops, a track maintenance crew up the line at Soldier Summit, above, unclogs the crossover at the west end of the yard in anticipation of the *Zephyr's* imminent passing.

M.P.

a proper ending

The track crew stands back to let the *Zephyr* and its miniature snowstorm sweep past. Below left, a white landscape becomes the stage and a silvery sky the backdrop as the dome obs tops the summit, its wheel clacks muffled by the powdery snow. *Silver Sky* serves as the perfect finale for the consist of the unique *Zephyr*. Whether viewed in early morning sunlight or the golden rays of a sunset, *Sky's* classic lines and interior appointments were unmistakable as that of another era.

M.P.

M.P.

The familiar covered wagon trio grinds up the middle tangent of Gilluly horseshoe loops under maximum load. Together the three reconditioned F's were limited to ten cars, and thanks to the train's increasing popularity, and with the addition of a business car, this maximum consist was not an uncommon sight later in the decade. In the winter months with the steam generator the count diminished to nine cars. On the facing page, the RGZ—looking much like the *California Zephyr* of later years what with a ten-car consist and flat-top cars next to the diner—speeds through Colton in 1974 with a GP40 subbing 5771 for additional horsepower.

M.P.

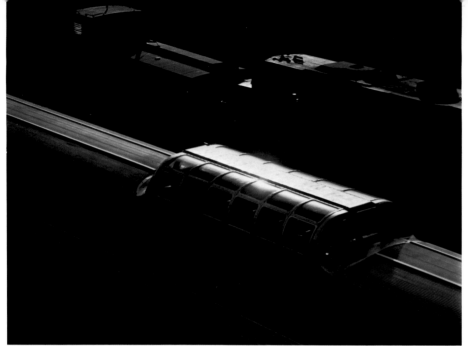

M.P.

chasing the sun

Sundown. We're in the mountain highlands and Salt Lake City draws near. The last dinner has been served and in the lounge passengers are making their final toasts to the remarkable train and the day's remarkable adventure. A toast to the *Zephyr:* Sail On Silver Girl!

M.P.

By the time No. 17 chased the sun through Spanish Fork Canyon, facing page, the lounge and diner had closed and waiters and attendants were packed up and waiting in *Silver Banquet* for arrival in Salt Lake. At left, the conductor prepares to highball the near-empty train of his command out of Provo for the final sprint through the Mormon farmlands to Salt Lake City, where the day's closing scenes will be accomplished after dark.

four hours, four years

The D&RGW main line parallels that of Union Pacific for a few miles north of Provo. Here, in May 1980, the mid-continent rivals exercise their most effective public relations tools as the eastbound *Zephyr* highballs toward Utah's third largest city while four tracks over and four hours later, UP's famed 8444 likewise accelerates down the tangent to Provo on one of its typical excursion assignments. The existence of either train in the ninth decade of this century is equally remarkable. Interestingly, 8444 is regarded as a relic from another era, yet it is but four years older than the stainless-steel consist of today's *Zephyr*.

M.P.

This photographic journey ends at Rio Grande's depot in Salt Lake City. The ornate structure dates from 1910 and has witnessed the arrivals and departures of a multitude of *Exposition Flyers, Royal Gorges, Scenic Limiteds, California Zephyrs,* and, now, *Rio Grande Zephyrs.* Its edifice is in good repair and its spacious main passenger waiting room still performs the function for which it was intended; indeed, people were literally beating down the station's doors to book space aboard the *Zephyr.*

R.L.

M.P.

M.P.

As another dawn filters through the Wasatch peaks, familiar depot scenarios are enacted once more. Passengers and baggage are loaded aboard this last vestige of a romantic grand conveyance. "Grand Junction, Glenwood Springs, and Denver train this way." Another memorable day of good food, fine fellowship, and spell-binding vistas await.

The *Rio Grande Zephyr* was the last of the breed of passenger train whose equipment and services were tailored strictly to a given route. It's traditions and heritage survived from the fleet of "West Wind" trains that premiered with the *Pioneer Zephyr* of 1934, and by the 1980s the RGZ was a unique national asset, a rolling landmark. Missing were the Zephyrettes, private rooms, and Pullman blankets, but dining and lounge services continued and domes still taught *Zephyr* riders what scenery was all about. And most important, the public could still ride regularly scheduled passenger trains over the most scenic railroad route in the U.S. At right, rays of morning sunshine fall upon Denver-bound No. 18 as it eases away from Salt Lake City depot. The little *Zephyr* seems to beckon, "Ride again!" Rest assured, we will.

AFTER EMIGRATING to Colorado in 1973, Richard Loveman became infatuated with the *Rio Grande Zephyr* and the photographic possibilities of its route through Utah and his new home state. At first he viewed the passenger train as a leftover mutate of the *California Zephyr*; however, with the increasing standardization of Amtrak trains throughout the country, he soon came to recognize the *Zephyr* as a special entity in the World of the Seventies.

Born in New York City in 1948 and raised on Long Island, Rich graduated from the University of Pennsylvania, and after receiving his architecture degree from the University of California, returned East to marry his Philadelphia honey, Alice. Immediately they packed all their worldly belongings into their '66 Mustang and headed west. In time, Rich and Alice became the proud parents of two remarkable children, James and Clare.

Rich spent much of his first seven years of married life dragging members of the family on *Zephyr* photo outings that produced some "extraordinarily worthless" exposures. Determined toward more-successful results, the family repeatedly ventured out until they were able to capture the quality images necessary for a book like NEVER ON WEDNESDAY. Alice has learned to endure the frustrations of a malcontent husband; the kids know no better and think that Daddy is perfectly normal.

IN 1950 a six-year-old Chicago boy received his first toy train. From that day on, Mel Patrick has played with trains—only the scale has changed. While attending the University of Illinois and Northwestern University in the middle Sixties, Mel spent much of his spare time photographing passenger trains at downtown stations and refining an unusual synchronized flash system for action night photography.

Mel started his railroading career with Illinois Central in 1967 at the old office building above Central Station. He reminisces, "The railroad had no air-conditioning, used straight pins instead of paper clips, and ran many, many passenger trains. Shortly after I began working there, the railroad decided to use paper clips and stop running passenger trains." Mel pleads innocent.

After Army duties, Mel went to work for the Rock Island in 1972 and shortly thereafter—in the spirit of the *Zephyr* West Wind—transferred to Denver. The Rock declined pathetically over the next four years (Mel again pleads innocent) and in 1976 he moved over to Denver & Rio Grande Western.

In 1978 it finally dawned on Mel, as with Rich, that the *Rio Grande Zephyr* was a unique remnant of passenger train past as well as a unique experience in passenger train present. The two dedicated photographers and authors-to-be collaborated, and NEVER ON WEDNESDAY became a reality.

NEVER ON WEDNESDAY, *from the publishers of Passenger Train Journal*

PUBLISHED BY: PTJ Publishing Inc., Park Forest, Illinois
PUBLISHER: Kevin McKinney
BOOK EDITOR: Mike Schafer
CONSULTING EDITOR: Kevin Keefe
LAYOUT: Richard Loveman
DARKROOM WORK: Mel Patrick
ART PRODUCTION AND TYPOGRAPHY: Mike Schafer
TYPESETTING: Delzer Lithograph Company, Waukesha, Wisconsin
HALFTONES, PRINTING AND BINDING: Cal Press Graphics, El Monte, California